incorect poetry

An anthology of love, longing and loneliness

Volume VII

Copyright ©2019.
All rights reserved.
Volume 7 of 12.

www.incorectpoetry.com
Ig @incorect_poetry
incorectpoetry@gmail.com

incorect poetry Volumes 1 - 12
Available on Amazon

Mistakes were made in life, love, spelling and grammar.

Disclaimer:

Due to a filing error on our part the physical copy paper stock is different. Volume I - VII are on glossy stock and Volumes VII - XII plain stock. If you are unsatisfied, please reach out at the above email address.

Thank you

She is the broken

                            Mirror

            The shattered pieces

    Are but

                A reflection of herself

I wish
I hadn't fallen
In love with you
The way I did
Like a fool
Always ready to rush in
How I thought myself so heroic as a poet
A nobleman
Oh
How I thought these idle words
Would save you
I love you
And that was enough
Love without works
Is dead
But if I believe in it
It's true
Actuality it takes two
Can't have one sided love

I can fill the void
In your loneliness
But not the one in your heart

We can lay here lovelessly
As I try to fit square blocks
Into circular slots

It's funny
How we both
Have these heart shaped puzzles
In our chests

But neither of us
Have the missing pieces
To fit
Into the others heart

I can fill the void
In your loneliness

I invited her to the movies
But
She didn't see the sequel
And I
Wanted to see
The third part of a trilogy

I asked
What she watched on Netflix
We met before season 1
Both of us
Had already watched it
Binged it all the way through
But season 2
She'd been waiting for someone
Other than me to
Chill

Oh
How these words of affection
Would be more endearing
From another

And yet
I still
Tell her
I love her

Our pictures
May have never ended up
Inside of a locket
Because you never open up to anybody
Not even a locksmith
I'm sure you keep a piece of my heart
Beneath the lint in your pocket

I don't know the karma
Which suits you

Sometimes
I think I'm on the wrong side of poetry
To be the heartbreaker
Rather than to be the heartbroken
To have never had to turn the page
To be on the opposite side of the pen
Inflicting words
Due to conflicting emotions
To destroy by desire
Just as those who watch the flame
Can only get so close to the fire
To inspire and be a muse
But alas
I'd rather you not
Suffer such abuse

Let's just let this be it
Because neither one of us
Can seem to commit
Each of our desires
Seem to conflict
Cuz you want this
And I want that
And we can't find a happy medium
I'm still thinking of her
And you're still dreaming of him
We were comfortably numb
Only suitably for each other
When we wanted to cum
Numbers were only good enough
To be dialed
When stood up
And we had no one else to turn to
Booty calls
Are becoming more than usual
It's almost like we're a couple now
The way we end up with each other
Every other night
I'll be damned
If we were each other's rock
But at this point
It's getting too deep
And I think we should stop

I'm afraid
I'm at loves end
Because
I have done so many things
In the name of love
That I don't think
I'll ever be able to do them again
Only so many times
You can fall head-over-heels
Keep rotating
Through the same loveless clichés
I've given away so many firsts
Only for it to never last
As an open heart
Slowly closes
Here's another
Dozen roses

Good morning

I'm not sure if this message
Has any meaning
If you roll out of bed
Read it
And smile
Then it's worth
Every bit of sunshine
Or if I'm left on read
And you're still there
Just to roll back into bed
To continue on dreaming
Nevertheless
I'm going to make the effort anyway

Good night

You are the cat to my love
When you stand there
Meowing for attention
Even though I've already fed you
With every bit of my heart

You want attention
When you want attention
And you want it meow
But when I go to pet you
You want nothing to do with me

Turn your whiskers to the air
Ans walk away

It's 3 a.m.

And your weighing heavily
On my chest

You are the cat to my love

I would like to dance
With romance
Just once

Hold hands
At the top of the whole world
While we scream our undying love

To press my lips against a kiss
To have that one-night stand with that one night

Never to look back for the rest of my days
To give a dozen lovers a bouquet of roses
For none of it to make any sense

But still feel just right

```
We want love
In all the ways
We imagine
```

To love
Is the cruelest fate
When not reciprocated
It is the seed
Of the flower
Which anticipated
To be planted
Take root
Grow, wither and die
And yet
Here I am with a bouquet

I've been looking
For the anthology of love
The harmony in hugs
The caress of a kiss
To be in your embrace
Face to face
Nose to nose
Eyes closed
To be taken
By passion

I think
I'm in love again
But I don't want to be
Because from past experience
I know how this will end
In the least cliché way
What I thought would be a happy ending
Ended in heartbreak
So please excuse me
If I'm skeptical
As I protect the hole
Where my heart used to be
Because I thought it'd be harmless
If I left it unguarded
In the hands of another

What's worse
To lust
Or trust
To be vulnerable
Completely naked
Unclothed
With your heart on your sleeve
Down on your knees
Begging them to take it

What's worse
To trust
Or lust
To be vulnerable
Half-naked
Clothes on the bed
With my pants around my ankles
Down on your knees
For a job that's thankless

Her smile
Is most precious
Protect it
By any and all means

Love
Is in between
The moments
Before you even know
What's happening
In the center of the fold
Whilst everything is unraveling
It comes to fruition
Because you found
What you've been missing

To the hearts
I've held
Which have crumbled
In the palm of my hand
Not only to my own doing
But because
Of the fragile condition
They were given to me in
I tried to take the tattered
And fix the broken
But to what avail
If they have lost hope
To no longer believe
It exists in themselves
I am the boy
Who continues
To build sandcastles
In the rain

I want a love
Where I've seen
The sadness in your smile
The joy in your tears
Where we agree
To disagree
Before
I even walk out the door
You're already missing me
With your perfectly
Messed up mascara
You're beautifully ugly
When you scream
How much you hate me
I can hear
How much you actually love me

I want nothing more
Than to hold your hand
While we stare down
The apocalypse
To know
You'll be there
Until the end

```
Love
Through every change
Even if it means
Them leaving
```

Walking on embers
Through the fire
On all the jagged
Broken pieces of heart

I've been tumbling
Wondering
When I'll slip out
Of this endless spiral
Of denial
Love conquers all

To the little garden of words
Which my heart doesn't deserve
Because I'm partial to curse
Sweet nothings and empty promises
Is all that I'm worth

She said
I love you
It sounded so shallow
Yet I was immersed
Drowning

I'm just a penguin
With a pebble
And she likes skipping stones

Loves monetary value
Could explain
Why so many
Of us
Are broke